CW01080570

# Tiger Aries
## The Combined Astrology Series

Zakariya Adeel

The Combined Astrology Series
TIGER-ARIES
By Zakariya Adeel

ISBN: 1546863036
ISBN-13: 9781546863038

# DEDICATION

To all of the people I have met, liked, disliked, loved, despised…
you have all been intriguing to me and it has been my pleasure
learning from you so that I could complete this full series of the
144 archetypes. I dedicate your combined astrological archetype to
you. If I've read for you, even if I met you fleetingly, if you shared
your date of birth with me, you have probably been inspiration for
the book on your astrological combination as I have an exceptional
memory for people and their astrology.

The Combined Astrology Series
TIGER-ARIES
By Zakariya Adeel

The Combined Astrology Series
TIGER-ARIES
By Zakariya Adeel

# CONTENTS

# 1. THE YEAR OF THE TIGER

Fiery, wild and dramatic, the year of the Tiger promises excitement by the bucket load. Never content with the quiet life, the Tiger takes action to ensure life is full of glitter and gold, even if it means rocking the boat to get it. Emerging from the quiet and conservative Ox year, the shift to the Tiger influence can come as a bit of shock.

Rebellious, powerful and proud, the Tiger likes to have things his way and sets out to make it so. However, he makes impulsive decisions based upon whims rather than actual needs so is usually quite disappointed once the goal is reached. Even the more logical and emotionally aware signs will find this process in operation in Tiger years. It creates unnecessary obstacles, wastes time and more importantly, wastes mental energy on irrelevant matters. The Tiger and drama go hand in hand. Rarely will you find yourself bored in a Tiger year; you will be too busy trying to resolve the current palaver you are embroiled in.

Although he is a high achiever and secretly, a perfectionist, his overt priority is to have fun. And this will be a fun year. Lending everyone his magnetic charm and charisma, an environment for creative exploration is formed. How creative you want to be and in which area of your life is up to you. Relationships can be created and destroyed easily in this environment; though it is hard with this sexy Tiger influence, think through the potential consequences before you take any significant action. If your immediate priority is *fun*, then you're in for a grand time.

Traditionally, Tiger years are seen as turbulent and tumultuous where disagreements, rash behavior and collisions occur. It is an extreme sign so extreme conditions are to be somewhat expected. Politically, the atmosphere is charged and many secrets are uncovered that cause uproar. Even the weather tends to be dramatic.

On the other side of the coin, it is a year of innovation. The Tiger is bold enough to tread territory others are not. New controversial ideas are discussed and audacious decisions can be made to improve the lives of many especially those who have stagnated. Avoiding change is difficult in such an unconventional and unorthodox environment.

The Rat year offers vision, the Ox year provides intense labor to lay the foundations, the Tiger year lends Passionate Creativity; it is time to market and sell the product.

Keep your own counsel and use the Tiger's self-assurance to go it alone rather than joining with others in business ventures. This excess of energy can also be utilized to reinvigorate seemingly lost causes or failing industries. With the economic downturn slowly easing, an infusion of Tiger energy is exactly what is required to increase productivity and boost general confidence. A lot can be achieved in a short space of time but do not expect results immediately.

The Tiger likes to play and ultimately doesn't take life too seriously; if you keep this attitude too, the Tiger year could be a party of excessive indulgence. Just remember to consider the potential consequences.

This is the Year of the Tiger.

# 2 THE TIGER YEARS

01/26/1914-02/13/1915

02/13/1926-02/01/1927

01/31/1938-02/18/1939

02/17/1950-02/05/1951

02/05/1962-01/24/1963

01/23/1974-02/10/1975

02/09/1986-01/28/1987

01/28/1998-02/15/1999

02/14/2010-02/02/2011

02/01/2022-01/21/2023

# 3 THE TIGER SIGN

**Chinese Name: HU**

**Rank: 3rd**

**Hours Ruled: 3am – 5am**

**Direction: East – Northeast**

**Season: Winter**

**Month: February**

I am passion personified with more confidence than I can keep up with. Curiosity has nearly killed me a million times, but I'm quick on my paws and love the thrill of the game. Calm on the surface, a storm on the inside; nobody understands the enigma that I am, I feel so much, I care so much, but I need my freedom even more! Wealth, status or fame, rarely impress me as these cat-eyes see bullshit for bullshit. Earn my respect, give me the truth and I'll infuse you with my energy, a rush of a trillion stars that flow from my veins into yours. I can fuel you when you're depleted, I can excite you when drabness threatens: my aliveness revives even the dead. As a feral cat, expect the unexpected, but also know that what I really want is to be tamed... actually, I'll never be tamed but I'll let you think I am. I'm the impulsive, independent, improviser; the lone warrior, I trust myself and myself alone, even if I love you, I'll always be alone in my Tiger-ness, you wouldn't understand.

I am the Tiger.

Highly attractive and highly sexed with a massive need for attention. You strut about wearing the face of an all powerful predator yet in private, you suffer with extreme insecurity. Extroverted and captivating, you know how to allure your prey. Moving from one self-induced drama to the next, you spend your time in the midst of activity. You never stop, even when you should, but lucky for you, you have an abundance of energy to call upon. You also hold strong social and political beliefs for which you're not afraid to fight. Tigers have big, bold audacious personalities, even the quieter ones and like adrenaline pumping activities. Interestingly, many tigers have a severe fear of growing old and of death.

Career-wise, Tigers prefer to be independent of hierarchies and seek autonomy in their work life. They usually try to fit into corporate environments until that first sacrifice of their integrity, which shocks their stripes right off them. Then when the politics and backstabbing start, the Tiger ducks and dives for a bit until their intentions are misconstrued, work is ignored and honesty is taken advantage of. Then they're off. And they often choose to commit to their creative occupations, they commonly work as/in; musicians (often rock and folk), singer-songwriters, lawyers, sports, teachers, journalists, PR workers, military positions, and jobs within science and technology.

# 4 THE ARIES SIGN

**1st Sign of Zodiac**

**Modality: Cardinal**

**Element: Fire**

**Ruler: Mars**

**Season: Spring**

**Metal: Iron**

**Stone: Amethyst, Diamond**

**Color: Red**

**Anatomy: Head, face**

I am the rambunctious ram, Mars' child, raw electric energy. First born, born charging and charging to be first, win is what I do in every aspect of my life. Stirring in my gut is a volcano of emotion and it is not always easy for me to understand what it means. But I know what I want when I see it and it's mine before I've even finished my thought. I'll follow only until I am ready to lead. Competition only serves to remind me how extraordinary I am, though my daredevil antics often embroil me in complicated dramas. I act before I think. I want before it's time. I lose only the things I should have valued when they were mine. I live in the moment and thrive in the midst of action. Though I contemplate, the "Why's" stifle the inferno within; I let it go, so I can too.

I am Aries.

As the first sign of the Western zodiac, Aries sees itself as a little bit more important than everyone else, after all, it is first. As a result, they also tend to take on their fair share of responsibilities but do so with a "why do I have to do everything?" attitude. Well, if one volunteers for everything, that person will be given everything to handle. Although, they are organized and handle these responsibilities well, there is that side to them that they just like to moan about their perceived burdens, though it's more playful than serious. Actually, their infectious energy imbues everything they do and Aries people are a lot of fun to be around. It's a fire sign so it seems their energy is endless and they never run out of steam.

Aries is also one of the leaders of the zodiac and they cherish taking charge of people and situations. Let them make the plans and organize the people and they will be happy... that is as long as everyone toes the line. Disobedience is not appreciated. Being open and honest with them about your feelings is however and they usually reciprocate and are open to adjusting for reasonable and understandable objections.

As Aries is symbolized by the rambunctious Ram, it's emotional life seems to be raw and they have a visible vulnerability that many other signs lack. This is both a blessing and a curse. When added to a Chinese sign like Dog or Snake, it is a distinct advantage as it opens them up in a way that makes them more accessible. Generally, Aries express their feelings as they have them, then leave them behind and moves on with life taking every challenge as it comes. This is very healthy and serves them well. It is true, that they to can dwell on stuff, but this is not their natural inclination, but usually a learned, especially if they have a Virgo parent. Because of their emotional aliveness, they make very sensual lovers and know how to dance in-sync with their partner. Caring and sharing every moment, perhaps too much at times, but they like to make people feel safe in their love… however, there are those Aries that also know how to make the room cold and uninviting if it is their intention to freeze people out. Know that Aries have the secret to universal temperature control like Storm from the Xmen.

Aries people are like project managers of the world and love to get projects off the ground and love to get the input from others, working collaboratively to complete them. Multitalented though they are, they might only choose show two-dimensions of their character because they have reserved much of themselves only for their true loved ones. Wen they are low, their expression of their emotions and their personal brand of vulnerability serves them in ways they are usually completely oblivious to. This vulnerability juxtaposed by their strength is what makes the Aries so beautiful.

# 5 THE TIGER ARIES

**Western Zodiac Equivalent of Tiger: Aquarius**

**Aquarius Western Element: Air**

**Eastern Zodiac Equivalent of Aries: Dragon**

**Aries Western Element: Fire**

**Numerology: 25 = 7**

*"Failure has a thousand explanations. Success doesn't need one."*

**- Alec Guiness**

The Tiger's whirlwind meets Aries' raging fire to create a dramatic personality wearing its heart on its sleeve but locking the rest of the world in a cage to keep this precious heart protected somehow. Even though this is not possible, the Tiger-Aries simply cannot imagine locking themselves in a cage to keep themselves guarded, no, they have far too much life to live, but they are aware of their own vulnerable sensitivities so they'll attempt to claw the world into submission instead. But with the Tiger-Aries personality, the world enjoys every second of it.

First and foremost, this is a very honest combination. Yet, despite a strong desire to remain grounded, they allow the events of the external world to whip them up into a variety of frenzies that their friends and loved one's hear about. They often need to be calmed down and helped to return to a place of balance. They know what is happening, they can explain the psychological workings of the people involved along with their intentions, yet still their emotional reaction remains heightened. Some may suspect that this is typical Tiger attention seeking, but it is not. They just feel so intensely that their emotional-irrational adrenaline releasing functions cannot be over-ridden by their mental processes.

There is also a strange relationship with what they perceive as "flamboyancy." Whether they like it or not, there is something a little flamboyant about them; some accept it openly, Lady Gaga and Hugh Hefner, whereas others try to distance themselves. Alec Guiness said, "Flamboyance doesn't suit me. I enjoy being elusive." One does not necessarily negate the other. When they accept their naturally colorful nature, they tend to find authentic connection with their true inner diva.

Like many of the Tiger combinations, they can be obsessive perfectionists but do not want this to be known, instead they like

12

to present that everything they do comes easily and naturally. In all actuality, they have organised, plotted and planned every aspect of their act. But the world doesn't mind; it's a great show.

Tiger-Aries people have a fantastic ability to create worlds and draw people into them. Lady Gaga and Hugh Hefner are two examples of people who have this talent. Many are drawn to jobs where they are in charge of setting the parameters of the working environment. Being so emotionally led, they understand how to tug at other's heart strings also.

The women of this combination may be innocent looking yet hugely audacious. They might not have felt like the prettiest girl during childhood so they are determined to make up for it. Victoria Beckham and Lady Gaga both have said they struggled with their weight when they were younger. Maybe this is why there is real support from them for others to find their true beauty, to do whatever they have to in order to feel beautiful in every way. Lady Gaga has said, "Be yourself and love who you are and be proud. Because you were born this way, baby." She has also advised, "First thing in the morning, try to think compassionate thoughts about yourself for five minutes. I don't always do it, but I try to." Similarly, Leighton Meester said, "If you're just yourself, you'll never lose. I want to be myself. That's when you feel the most comfortable, that's when you have the most success, and that's when you're the most happy."

Natural performers, these women know how to captivate their prey. It was Victoria Beckham who chased down her hubby-to-be David Beckham (Rabbit-Taurus) in a very calculated way; she attended the football (soccer) match with the sole goal to attract his attention and she asked him out. Regardless of their chosen field, they are always comediennes first and know how to lighten the mood of any situation. Amanda Bynes has said, "I think I grew up sort of admiring comedians and I grew up watching the greats. And so my dad was really supportive of me doing this."

The men of this combination are just as ostentatious as their female counterparts despite their protestations. Hugh Hefner has said, If there was going to be a sexual revolution, I would be its pamphleteer." Usually, the men feel like stolid dorks on the inside, so they spend much of their time pursuing more exciting activities in the external world. Spending more time looking at who they actually are and how well this matches up to the image they actually would like to be, tends to be helpful.

Being as honest as they are, they are not afraid of sharing their opinions, even if they may be deemed as controversial. They would consider themselves "sexually liberated" even if their ideas of what this actually is may differ. Hugh Hefner has said, "The major civilizing force in the world is not religion, it's sex... The part of the women's movement that was anti-sexual was ill-conceived" Whereas Lady Gaga has said, "In my opinion, the last thing a young woman needs is another picture of a sexy pop star writhing in sand, covered in grease, touching herself.... I hope that young women know that sex is still a big deal, and they don't have to put out soon. If they want someone to court them for a while before they give it up, that's wonderful and beautiful, and a man will only respect you more for honoring your body. I am that way." That being said, Jenna Jameson is also a Tiger Aries born on the same day as Hugh Hefner, 9th April. She has said, "I try my hardest to push the point that I am a feminist. I really think it's important that people know that the women in this industry are empowered. They run it, man. It's awesome." Three different views of sex, yet all three of them claim sexual empowerment. It's very Tiger-Aries!

This particular brand of Tiger is especially emotion-led and loves to be this way despite what they say. Alyson Hannigan has said "You need to suffer to be interesting." It is probably true that those who have been through great adversity have a fuller, rounder character; although law of attraction suggests this sort of view held firmly in mind may attract complicated drama's to the belief bearer. The Tiger Aries Artist lives for these experiences so that they can draw from them honestly and with detailed precision. Being of the brave variety, they would rather make the mistake than regret anything. They push boundaries and dare more than most, yet still they feel like they haven't done enough. Alec Guiness said, "I have only one great regret - that I never dared enough. If at all." If they do not get the support they require from the powers that be, they will just go out there and create their dreams solo. Lady Gaga has said, "If I have any advice to anybody, it's to just do it yourself, and don't waste time trying to get a favor."

Their eternal search for meaning is unlikely to end because they are rarely still enough to catch up with themselves. The Aries fire heats this whirlwind to the point that they keep floating higher and higher into the stratosphere. But instead of looking where they are going, they can't take their eyes off the ground.

# 6 FAMOUS TIGER ARIES'

**Jann Arden**

**Elle Fanning**

**Alyson Hannigan**

**Amanda Bynes**

**Leighton Meester**

**Matthew Broderick**

**Tricia Helfer**

**Marley Shelton**

**Peyton List**

**Alec Guinness**

**Jenna Jameson**

**Lady Gaga**

Martin Short

Clark Gregg

Claudia Cardinale

William Sadler

Edgar Wright

Marcia Cross

Rosie O'Donnell

Hugh M. Hefner

Victoria Beckham

David Cassidy

Agnetha Fältskog

# 7 COMPATIBILITIES

| | |
|---|---|
| Soul Mate: | Boar-Virgo |
| Siblings: | Tiger-Leo, Tiger-Sagittarius |
| Best Friends: | Horse-Aries, Horse-Leo, Horse-Sagittarius, Dog-Aries, Dog-Leo, Dog-Sagittarius |
| Good Friends: | Rabbit-Taurus, Rabbit-Virgo, Rabbit -Capricorn, Sheep-Taurus, Sheep-Capricorn, Boar-Taurus, Boar -Virgo, Boar –Capricorn |
| Avoid: | Rat-Gemini, Rat-Libra, Rat-Aquarius, Dragon-Gemini, Dragon-Libra, Dragon-Aquarius, Monkey-Gemini, Monkey-Aquarius |
| Challenger: | Monkey-Libra |

# Soul Mate & Challenger Matches

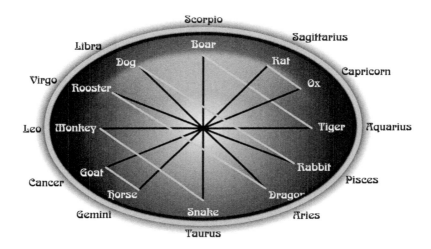

Looking at the Chinese Sign chart first, trace your way along the WHITE line starting at your sign to the other end; this sign is your Chinese sign's Soul Mate sign. Then do the same thing with your Western Zodiac sign and put these two signs together. For example, taking the RAT-ARIES:

The RAT's Soul Mate is the OX.

The ARIES' Soul Mate is VIRGO.

Therefore, the Soul Mate combination for the RAT-ARIES is OX-VIRGO.

Interestingly, if you follow the BLACK lines to each sign's polar opposite sign, you will find your opposing "Challenger" combination, which is seen as the combination that is the most difficult for you to get along with. However, it is exceptionally common for people to be drawn to their Challenger combination as it creates a life full of ups and downs. As the old proverb goes: opposites attract. See if it is true for you too.

Again using RAT-ARIES as an example:

The RAT's opposite sign is the HORSE.

The ARIES' opposite sign is LIBRA.

Therefore, the Opposite or "Challenger" combination for the RAT-ARIES is HORSE-LIBRA.

# Best Friend Matches

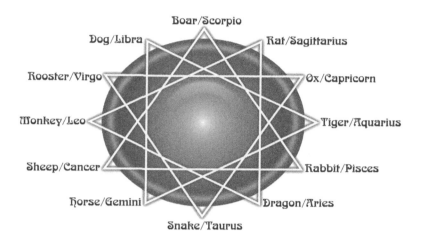

Each of the 144 combinations can be broken down into 16 groups of nine signs. The inhabitants of each group share similarities: attributes, traits, tastes, working environments, strengths, weaknesses, they may even have similar value systems. Traditional Chinese Astrologers recommend you select your friends and partner from either your soul mate signs or your best friend group as they will be most compatible for your individual combination.

See below for your best friend matches.

Achievers

With a large presence and a big personality they instinctively know how to get the best out of others. It's important for them to think big and nurture their vision as these are the elite when it comes to material achievement. With an abundance of the positive Yang polarity, these types can be infused with a somewhat masculine energy. They are also: proactive, strong, overpowering, persuasive, objective, logical, unemotional, direct, harsh and miserly.

Relationship – Physical and experimental, these Alpha types have high emotions and sometimes explosive actions. A strong, power couple.

| | | |
|---|---|---|
| Rat-Aries | Dragon-Aries | Monkey-Aries |
| Rat-Leo | Dragon-Leo | Monkey-Leo |
| Rat-Sagittarius | Dragon-Sagittarius | Monkey-Sagittarius |

Mediators

Psychologically advanced, they are highly self-aware and have a superior understanding of human behavior. Their skills are best utilized in a social environment but do well in almost any job involving people and have an eye for detail. Modest and fair, they like to serve the needs of others altruistically and subsequently hold a lot of social clout. They are also: objective, understanding, honorable, careful, fussy, pessimistic, worriers and security conscious.

Relationship - Based upon mutual respect and understanding, long conversations, hugs and sensual activities.

| | | |
|---|---|---|
| Rat-Taurus | Dragon-Taurus | Monkey-Taurus |
| Rat-Virgo | Dragon-Virgo | Monkey-Virgo |
| Rat-Capricorn | Dragon-Capricorn | Monkey-Capricorn |

Sirens

Physically attractive and vain, they present themselves well and are mentally astute. With big ego's they like to garner attention without making it obvious. Making money is no problem as they know precisely what they can do and how it can be marketed to best effect. Romantic and evocative, they like to chase and be chased equally. They can also be: soppy, clever, artistic, alternative, rebellious, loners, and innovative.

Relationship – With tons of sex appeal, both partners are always in demand. Competitive and egotistical, both may have a long list of previous conquests.

| Rat-Gemini | Dragon-Gemini | Monkey-Gemini |
|---|---|---|
| Rat - Libra | Dragon-Libra | Monkey-Libra |
| Rat-Aquarius | Dragon-Aquarius | Monkey=Aquarius |

Motivators

Getting people on side and working collaboratively is their biggest skill. They know how to use their personality, sexuality and personal attributes to get ahead in a professional capacity. Working as an intermediary or in middle management appeals because this level of authority offers them the sort of affirmation they seek from staff and seniors. They are also: attention-seeking, secretly controlling, money motivated and have good memories.

Relationship – Will look to each other for support, encouragement and fulfillment. Like to serve each other's personal needs.

| Rat-Cancer | Dragon-Cancer | Monkey-Cancer |
| --- | --- | --- |
| Rat-Scorpio | Dragon-Scorpio | Monkey-Scorpio |
| Rat-Pisces | Dragon-Pisces | Monkey-Pisces |

Powerhouses

Strong and quiet unless roused. Self-confident and powerful, they like to take charge and see the situation through to a conclusion. Their internal strength attracts people and they are likely to wield a lot of influence. Challenge the Powerhouses at your peril, their bark is bad; their bite is worse. They are also: arrogant, deceptive, private, selfish, authoritative, dictatorial and have difficulty showing their affection.

Relationship – May have conventionally defined roles. Both need a lot of love but will not like this to be known.

| Ox-Aries | Snake-Aries | Rooster-Aries |
| --- | --- | --- |
| Ox-Leo | Snake-Leo | Rooster-Leo |
| Ox-Sagittarius | Snake-Sagittarius | Rooster-Sagittarius |

Perfectionists

A concentration of Yin energy here creates a cerebral and caring person first and foremost. However, nit-picking, moaning and being dissatisfied are favorite pastimes. Work is very important and they are usually well regarded. Physically, they like to take good care of themselves and if they do not, there are repressed feelings or emotional issues present. They like to present an image of being cool, calm and collected, but inside they are busy worrying whether this image is coming over or not. They are also: analytical, highly numerate, have large general knowledge, get embarrassed easily and are known for their quirky personalities and sense of humor.

Relationship – They have a big need to talk so they will have to learn to take turns. There's nothing they're not good at.

| Ox-Taurus | Snake-Taurus | Rooster-Taurus |
|-----------|--------------|----------------|
| Ox-Virgo | Snake-Virgo | Rooster-Virgo |
| Ox-Capricorn | Snake-Capricorn | Rooster-Capricorn |

Mentors

Leading by example, the Mentors walk the walk in order to talk the talk. Inspiring others is their biggest pay off. Although naturally self-absorbed, they have the mental stability to become aware of it and are usually are able to achieve a healthy balance. They make great teachers and loyal friends. Success seems to comes to them easily but make no mistake, they will have earned their worth.

Relationship – Forever learning, together they get better and better as they age.

| Ox-Gemini | Snake-Gemini | Rooster-Gemini |
|-----------|--------------|----------------|
| Ox-Libra | Snake-Libra | Rooster-Libra |
| Ox-Aquarius | Snake-Aquarius | Rooster-Aquarius |

The Gifted

With creative abilities and a rare mental dexterity, they excel in any occupation they choose. Confident and attractive, they are never short of admirers, although they tend to be picky when selecting a partner. They are also: precious, humble, romantic, rhythmical, open and spiritual.

Relationship – They seek someone equally attractive and with a high status or high self-worth which will eventually unfold in high status. Both will find deep respect for each other.

| | | |
|---|---|---|
| Ox-Cancer | Snake-Cancer | Rooster-Cancer |
| Ox-Scorpio | Snake-Scorpio | Rooster-Scorpio |
| Ox-Pisces | Snake-Pisces | Rooster-Pisces |

Storytellers

With their heart on their sleeves they go through life learning its lessons and then they will turn it into a beautiful story to share with the world. Striving always to keep their feet on the ground, they observe the world through an artistic lens and articulate their feelings truthfully. They are also: honest, rebellious, popular, energetic, attractive, particular and demanding.

Relationship – highly sexed and with a thirst for new experiences, life with a storyteller is never dull. Together, they keep each other forever entertain in every way possible.

| | | |
|---|---|---|
| Tiger-Aries | Horse-Aries | Dog-Aries |
| Tiger-Leo | Horse-Leo | Dog-Leo |
| Tiger-Sagittarius | Horse–Sagittarius | Dog-Sagittarius |

Genius'

Hiding behind their big personalities and sense of humor are the Genius'. Is there anything they don't know? Along with a highly evolved mind comes a self-importance. Riding the fine line between supreme self-confidence and extreme insecurity, they question whether they really are that advanced. They are also: self-effacing, organized, humorous, well-loved yet egotistical, misunderstood and often misconstrued.

Relationship - Few understand their plight. That's why they stick together and make a very loyal union.

| | | |
|---|---|---|
| Tiger-Taurus | Horse-Taurus | Dog-Taurus |
| Tiger-Virgo | Horse-Virgo | Dog-Virgo |
| Tiger-Capricorn | Horse-Capricorn | Dog-Capricorn |

Activists

With a nose for justice and a fearless attitude, Activists fight to create change and promote equality. This is the second grouping of concentrated Yang energy which gives them a strong sense of purpose, forward motion and confidence with which to proceed. Highly effective and sometimes forceful personalities, it may come as a surprise that they have a need for external affirmation to convince them that their ideals are worth striving for. They are also: attractive, single-minded, just, stubborn, diva-esque, selfish and may come across as insensitive when they offer their objective opinion.

Relationship – Faithful and true, this is one of the most attractive groups with spicy personalities so the partnerships range from juicy to volatile but never boring.

| Tiger-Gemini | Horse-Gemini | Dog-Gemini |
| Tiger-Libra | Horse-Libra | Dog-Libra |
| Tiger-Aquarius | Horse-Aquarius | Dog-Aquarius |

## Specialists

Whether they have studied a specific subject or not, they have a great deal of knowledge and information about specialist or niche subjects tucked away in their meticulous minds. It is for this reason they should work in an environment that stimulates them as their contribution can be vast and it does wonders for their confidence. Essentially, they are loners but may not seem such. Many are thrust into a position of leadership when it is may not actually be what they want. They are also: aloof, talented, humble, awkward, quiet, geeky, chameleons, addictive, private, abrupt and self-centered.

| Tiger-Cancer | Horse-Cancer | Dog-Cancer |
| Tiger-Scorpio | Horse-Scorpio | Dog-Scorpio |
| Tiger-Pisces | Horse-Pisces | Dog-Pisces |

## Aesthetics

Graceful and charming, Aesthetics' are on a search for inner and outer beauty. Fashionable and delectable, they make everyone they come in contact with fall in love with them. Many will be found in creative work environments, especially show business. They are also: sweet, sexy, clever, emotional, open, caring, narcissistic, moody and secretive.

Relationship – It's important that both maintain a sense of who they are as individuals because it's easy for each to get lost in the other, not knowing where one begins and the other ends. A very sexy coupling none the less.

| Rabbit-Aries | Sheep-Aries | Boar-Aries |
|---|---|---|
| Rabbit-Leo | Sheep-Leo | Boar-Leo |
| Rabbit-Sagittarius | Sheep-Sagittarius | Boar–Sagittarius |

Intuitives

When the caring and creative energies of these Chinese signs meet the practicality of the Zodiac earth signs, we get a bunch of insightful, discerning and somewhat psychic group of types. They know how to make a profit and save money by accurately predicting future events. Their minds understand patterns so what has happened before suggests what is yet to come if you know how to read the events. They are also: spiritual, fun, lively, active, thorough, compassionate, emotional, unpredictable, domestic, neurotic and more detached than they seem.

Relationship – They know they must be open and honest with one another as there will be little the other will not read in their behavior. Luckily both are naturally loyal and monogamous when settled.

| Rabbit-Taurus | Capricorn | Sheep-Capricorn |
|---|---|---|
| Rabbit-Virgo | Sheep-Taurus | Boar-Taurus |
| Rabbit- | Sheep-Virgo | Boar-Virgo |

Boar-Capricorn

## Immortals

Innocent and free spirited their light and airy persona belies their true intelligence. Happy go lucky doesn't necessarily equal naivety, in fact they have good understanding of the universal laws which gives them their ethereal wisdom. Many may come across as hippy's promoting free love and joy. They are also: giving, non-judgmental, loving, generous, fun, optimistic, childish, forgetful, uncommitted, docile and prone to playing upon others expectations of them.

Relationship – Play and escapism will be important as will travel, and the feeling of freedom. Both will provide that for each other but will need to learn how to be serious also when the situation requires it.

| | | |
|---|---|---|
| Rabbit-Gemini | Sheep-Gemini | Boar-Gemini |
| Rabbit-Libra | Sheep-Libra | Boar-Libra |
| Rabbit-Aquarius | Sheep-Aquarius | Boar-Aquarius |

## Refined Sophisticate

Proper and gracious, they have a positive opinion of themselves and for good reason. They are talented, affable, amusing and understand their worth. They like the finer things in life and do not settle for second best. Not afraid of hard work, they will do what is necessary to sustain their high standards and image. Despite all of this, they are actually more vulnerable then they would ever admit. They are also: tender hearted, gentle, image-conscious, firm, level-headed, focused, pretentious, argumentative, proud and superior.

Relationship – Sensual and loving, both will dote on each other and may see themselves as a unit. Sociable and affectionate as a couple.

| | | |
|---|---|---|
| Rabbit-Cancer | Sheep-Cancer | Boar-Cancer |
| Rabbit-Scorpio | Sheep-Scorpio | Boar-Scorpio |
| Rabbit-Pisces | Sheep-Pisces | Boar-Pisces |

# 8 THE 12 TIGER COMBINED ASTROLOGY ARCHETYPES

When the 12 Chinese signs meet the 12 Western signs, both signs meet, converge and become affected by the others traits. In effect, there are 12 different types of each Chinese and Western signs which make up the 144 Combined Astrology Archetypes. Below is an introduction to each of this sign's 12 Archetypes.

For greater detail, please obtain "Secrets of the Combined Astrology." For more information, please visit: www.adeelsastrology.com

Tiger – Aries

The Tiger's whirlwind meets Aries' raging fire to create a dramatic personality wearing its heart on its sleeve but locking the rest of the world in a cage to keep this precious heart protected somehow. Even though this is not possible, the Tiger-Aries simply cannot imagine locking themselves in a cage to keep themselves guarded, no, they have far too much life to live, but they are aware of their own vulnerable sensitivities so they'll attempt to claw the world into submission instead. But with the Tiger-Aries personality, the world enjoys every second of it. Jann Arden has said, "To not think of dying, is to not think of living."

Tiger – Taurus

When the Tiger's tornado meets the Taurean's tough earth, it creates a personality that is unapologetic in being who it is. The Taurus allows the Tiger to run wild and do so with abandon so people with this combination are naturally uninhibited and it is a beautiful thing to observe. However, it can also be quite threatening to family structures, organized religions or such similar groups where too much freedom or sexual expression requires reining in. A Tiger's nature can never be contained for long and when it breaks free, guilt, shame and all manner of unhelpful emotions can cause them to jump back and forth from wildness to over-civilized-mildness until they recognize the socialized conditioning for what it is and eventually strike a healthier balance. Then they can run wild with control – it sounds like a paradox but Tiger people will understand. Queen Elizabeth II has said, "It's all to do with the training: you can do a lot if you're properly trained."

Tiger – Gemini

When the Tiger's tempest meets Gemini's inconstant cyclone it creates a personality that tends to live in the clouds. They have high expectations of themselves and of others even though they are unlikely to directly impose their views. They are too polite. But that does not mean that they do not think it. They have a winner's mentality and are happy to go out and make their dreams a reality regardless of how seemingly impossible. In fact, on some level they get a real kick out of it: the more difficult the better. Bring it on! Paula Abdul has said, "When you wish upon a star, you just might become one."

## Tiger – Cancer

When the Tiger's tempest meets Cancer's deep water, the result is a driven, humble and self-sufficient creature. With enough self-assurance to go it alone, they take risks and work ridiculously hard to ensure that their risks work out. And they usually do. Business is first on their minds, sex is second. Of course family is very important but with an ego that needs constant feeding, self preservation, elevation and freedom are prerequisites required to provide them with enough comfort before they set off to start a family that they can serve. On the surface, it may look selfish but it is anything but; if you do not give to yourself first, what will you have to give? In fact they are highly likely to be philanthropists. Their moral code is well developed much like all Tigers' but with Cancer blended in, they are also leaders, albeit of the shy variety.

## Tiger – Leo

When the Tiger's tornado mixes with Leo's blazing fire, the sparks fly so far and so high, they can be seen in outer space. This is the only double feline combination of all 144 combinations; the Tiger is like a smooth warrior and the Leo is the royal ruler so when they merge, one may expect to see a somewhat alpha personality. This is sort of accurate, but not in an in-your-face way. Subtlety is the Tiger's specialism and with the additional Leo power here, this creature knows how to get their way without directly asking for it. But that doesn't mean that they will manipulate, just because they can. It's enough for them to know that they have that weapon as part of their arsenal; for the most part they are led by an inner core of genuine integrity ...with a little ego thrown in. Usain Bolt has said, "If I get to be a legend, I've achieved my goal."

Tiger – Virgo

When the Tiger's tempest merges with Virgo's fertile earth, this personality is gifted with focus and clarity at the same time. Virgo's earthiness lends the ability to channel the force of the Tiger's storm in productive directions so that they are always working towards achieving some goal. To the outside, people with this combination seem very lucky with money. To call it luck is to denigrate and undermine the work of this creature. As Dr Phil has said, "The most you get is what you ask for." And they have no qualms about asking for more. They are good money makers because they like the feeling of financial security. They go with their hunches, research to expand their understanding and then work around the clock until they have achieved their objective. That's why they are always "lucky" with money. They make it happen.

Tiger – Libra

When the Tiger's tempest meets Libra's cool calm breeze, the result is an unconventional, vibrant creature that lives off its wits and is guided strongly by its instincts. Not that the Tiger-Libra always listens, but they do kick themselves afterwards;

when they know better, they want to do better, but don't always have the confidence to see this through; at least until the universe demands it of them which they often learn the hard way. Unlike the snake sign that needs to project an image to the outside world while knowing who they actually are within, the Tiger will justify the existence of any chosen image regardless whether the external world sees this image or not. That does not mean that they don't care what others think, they do, in fact they lose a lot of sleep over what people are going to think or say about them, but they need to be seen as "good people" to themselves, whatever that means. This aspect of the airy Tiger is magnified when joined with airy Libra. Louise Hay has said, "As my mind can conceive of more good, the barriers and blocks dissolve. My life becomes full of little miracles popping up out of the blue."

Tiger – Scorpio

When the Tiger's tempest meets with Scorpio's dark murky waters, the result is an exuberant life-loving beast that gluttonously feasts on all manner of worldly delights before wearing itself out requiring solitude to recuperate its energies so that it can get out there and devour life all over again. Determined, intelligent and highly attractive, these felines know how to make things happen and function best in a sort of contained chaos that they know how to create and manage, even if nobody else does. There is a noted tendency towards a sort of hibernation every now and then because they need solace and time to get their heads right about the drama that ensues around them. Jodie Foster has said, "It's an interesting combination: Having a great fear of being alone, and having a desperate need for solitude and the solitary experience. That's always been a tug of war for me."

Tiger – Sagittarius

When the Tiger's tempest meets the Centaurs frisky fires, wildness meets cultivated civility, restlessness meets drive, subconscious merges with conscious with effortless ease. These people are constantly in communication with their inner selves and take intuitive, inspired action most of the time without their even being aware of it. That is why things work out for them even in the midst of chaos in fact, oftentimes, that is when they will function at their best. It is a good thing, for although they have an amazing ability to focus, as all Tigers do, this combination may prefer physical exercise or dance or movement based yoga as well as traditional meditation forms as a spiritual practice. This beast knows it needs to self-tame but must find a method it enjoys. Ralph Fiennes said, "I'm not very good at being domesticated. I've tried. The domestic life I find claustrophobic - the rituals and habits and patterns."

Tiger – Capricorn

When the Tiger's tempest meets with Capricorn's fertile earth, the storm pulls this creature to the skies while the earth pulls it down which causes some internal friction in the early years for people of this combination. This starts them on their ever-intensifying search for personal authenticity. When they choose to take charge and consciously decide to pick the particulars of their life, their natural power returns and lots of little things begin to happen which serve as symbols that they are heading in the right direction. As Eartha Kitt said, "The river is constantly turning and bending and you never know where it's going to go and where you'll wind up."

Tiger – Aquarius

When the Tiger's tempest meets Aquarius' cyclone, the resulting hurricane is mammoth. The Tiger and Aquarius are each other's east-west equivalent so in effect we have the pure Tiger or double Aquarius combination here. This means that the traits of the Tiger and of Aquarius are amplified which is really interesting considering what those traits are. Tiger's are fearless fighters of freedom, Aquarians are humanitarians with an eccentric bent led by their heart anywhere they please regardless how alternative. It is very easy to say that they are likely to be unusual in many regards, compassionate and ahead of their time by a century or two. The first image that crops up is the alternative rock/folk artist, casually strumming away with a few simple words of poetry that speaks millions. It comes as no surprise that this combination is jam-packed with singer-songwriters, writers and artists of all varieties.

Tiger – Pisces

When the Tiger's tempest meets the potency of Pisces' water, the result is raw sex appeal and a commitment to make manifest the art that lives in their soul. Many have exceptionally special looks. They stick out even from the good-looking crowd because they are more than just attractive, they are powerfully sexually appealing. Perhaps it is because they blessed thus, that they value relationships more than merely chasing sensual highs. Pisces' water opens the airy Tiger's mind so that psychology becomes much more important. These types seem to know what they want from a young age, why they want it and how they are going to get it. In order to be work focused, they often have to fight their

Tiger tendency to want to indulge in ego-serving play and ending up in complicated emotional situations. Eva Mendes said, "The celebrity world can be so ugly. Everyone seems to have slept with everyone else and it's some sort of strange weird cycle. I don't want to get into that."

# 9 THE 12 YEAR CYCLE PREDICTIONS FOR THE TIGER

Year of the Rat

A significant obstacle is removed from your path in the early part of this year however this does not give you the right to run wild. Consider the effect your actions have on others and try to tame your ego. It may not be the best year to make risky investments or set unrealistic goals. Self-delusion rarely pays off in the year of the rat. It is wiser to save your money for the future, think carefully about commitments and avoid impulsive behavior. Although it looks like money is flowing in from all sides, it is unlikely to last and expecting it to is immature. Planning ahead, keeping your own counsel and concentrating on your previous successes keeps you moving along productively. A slow yet eventful year lay in store where you will be challenged and pushed to advance. Your successes may equal your disappointments but you will emerge stronger and more powerful than before.

Year of the Ox

Being the impetuous carnivore that you are, you do not like being told what to do, how to do it or having time frames imposed upon you. This is why you may have difficulty in retaining a balanced perspective. Avoid hot-headed behaviour and realise that you must seem rational in order to be taken seriously and have your opinion heard. Ensure you are aware of all the facts so you have clarity of mind and can argue your side objectively. It would be prudent to avoid getting drawn into emotional battles and instead, focus on your achievements and successes. This will propel you down more productive routes and channel your energy effectively. Recognise that you always have the ability to choose your response to any stimulus.

Year of the Tiger

Welcome to your home ground. You've created the perfect environment in which to flourish. Funding will be available for you to undertake projects you've long planned for and you will feel somewhat protected by the well-wishers that surround you. As gracious Host, you may be expected to lend your presence to many social gatherings and loved ones will also make demands of your time. Give yourself the nurturance you need and do not let all of your activity lead you to exhaustion. If you have considered leaving a situation, possibly a job or relationship but circumstances have been complicated, the beginning of a resolution is in sight. This is going to be a busy year so get the personal organizer ready.

Year of the Rabbit

Prospects look good as the Rabbit lays a trail of goodies for you to collect along your journey back home to the Jungle now that your official rein is over. It is an encouraging year for your business and romantic endeavors. You may at times feel like you are not getting the attention you deserve or that you are expending a lot of energy for too few rewards. Consider whether this is a pre-established pattern of thinking rather than a response to any immediate stimuli. This is one of the best years for self-help and personal development, especially for signs that are that way oriented such as yours. Use the prevalent ethereal energies to highlight, deconstruct, understand then displace any negative notions by replacing them with positive ones. Spend much of your time in meditative pursuits if necessary. Affirmations and Visualizations undertaken with emotion will make you want to take constructive action. Then the miracles begin.

Year of the Dragon

Uncertainty and finding yourself in a tornado of activity keeps you on tenterhooks for the early part of the year. It might be hard to get a project off the ground or find funding. Sometimes things do not ignite for a reason. Although you do not mind going with the flow and adjusting to changes, they may come out of the left field and knock you off your feet. This you do not appreciate. Get back up and go with it. Partake in and enjoy the celebrations the Dragon lays out, but avoid trying to steal the spotlight, the Dragon alone will choose when and where the sun will shine. You will get your moment as long as you do not try to force it. Dragon years are not particularly comfortable for Tigers as there tends to be some sort of separation that they have to deal with, usually towards the end of the year. Allow yourself to renew your spirit, spend time with friends and you will find the inspiration you seek. This will herald the beginning of a new empowered you. Then you will set off to realize your new goals.

## Year of the Snake

It hasn't been easy for you to keep going when the rewards you believed you deserved were not commensurate with the work you were putting in: but that is all about to change under the Serpent's rule. The pace of everything speeds up and you may find that you will naturally start streamlining your life; the unnecessary will fall away, possibly through arguments or disagreements, but it will not be of any consequence because your focus will be on more important matters. Many synchronistic events and amazing coincidences take place and you appreciate every blessing. The autumn will be especially significant for you where you might win an award or get some sort of recognition. Although there is a lone warrior feel to this year, you bathe in your own glorious energy which replenishes you and those who serve your cause time and time again until success is in your Tiger paws.

## Year of the Horse

With a lightness of attitude, an ideology and set of values that is similar to that of the Horse, you find its years very easy to navigate. On top of all that, you are great pals with the Horse and are openly welcomed to the stable party. This year is full of positive surprises, gifts and adrenaline pumping activities that are right up your tiger alley. Professional and personal connections are easily made that elevate your position especially when you seek to further your philanthropic profile. Obtaining recognition for your efforts comes effortlessly and you seem to be a magnet for money in this year. The key to all of this is shifting your self-perception; the more you love and nurture yourself, the universe reciprocates in kind and adds power to your own self-love. Be as loving, giving and as generous as you can to others and to yourself.

Year of the Sheep

Having gotten used to the Horse's energy that suits yours so perfectly, your professional and personal goals may be progressing well, but as the energy shifts to that of the Sheep's, you may begin to feel a little disoriented. The Sheep does not like schedules or plans so will not respect yours, be ready and prepared to improvise. From May to September, a complicated situation that requires real inner strength may present itself. The more you know yourself the better, as you will need to rely on your personal wisdom. This time may force into undertaking some detailed analysis and self-work that you may have been running from for a good few years. Not on the Sheep's watch. What you learn at this time will be the reason the last phase of the year is so successful for you. Know that you do not need to be the center of attention al of the time in order to be popular or productive.

Year of the Monkey

As your opposite year, some friction is only to be expected, but it is interesting that through these obstacles, the Monkey furnishes you with opportunities galore. Not one to sit down and accept failure, you may find that you actually thrive through this time that astrologers would tell you is the nadir of the cycle for your sign. You have that Tiger spirit to thank for that. Through the various issues that you will face, your mind is set on success so you emerge stronger with an even larger fan base. You may actually feel empowered in this year and find that you can create miracles out of thin air. The Monkey likes to tease and toy with everyone that he feels could be competition, but there is also an underlying respect for anyone who takes up his challenge. As you continue to do that, you will find Tiger-treats that the imp has buried all over its Monkey mansion.


## Year of the Rooster

Put your roller skates on dear Tiger because it's a year where you will be continuously on the move. There is such momentum behind you that there might be times when you want to slow down or stop just to catch your breath. There will much change for you to deal with and it is wise to accept the circumstances and just go along with them, you will eventually be lead to wonderful new opportunities. It may feel like the old you is being broken down, fragmented into pieces that you will then organize into two sections: what works and what doesn't. This might also be the year where you learn to stop repressing those areas of your life that you are ashamed of or run from, repression will find expression in your Rooster year and then you will have to deal with it. Let what is illusory fall away and rebuild upon a foundation that is secure.


## Year of the Dog

The dog creates an environment in which you flourish. The barriers come down for you and the world becomes your oyster. Your career prospects look good and your money situation could finally stabilize, it's a good year for a relationship to mature or if you're still playing, you can expect to play hard. Luck protects the tiger folk this year, although still prone to the odd bout of depression from imagined loneliness, you are likely to find influential associates if you remember to work hard.


## Year of the Boar

You may have met many influential people last year and have organized some mutually beneficial arrangements that may have paid off. Because of this, you may be tempted to continue in this vain and this is where you must be careful. Check the details, fine print and people attached before committing especially if it looks too good to be true. If it all looks kosher, then proceed with every ounce of your energy because financial gains can be huge this year as long as you adopt a business outlook as well as a creative one.

For all the 144 Archetypes, check out:
Secrets of the Combined Astrology

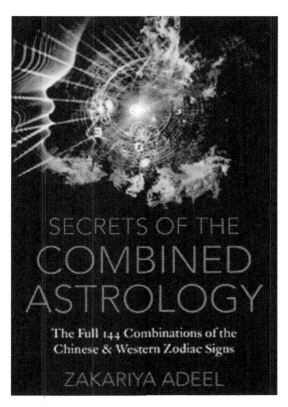

www.adeelsastrology.com

Buy from:

UK Amazon

US Amazon

Printed in Great Britain
by Amazon